curious NATURE

Q&A ABOUT

THE HUMAN BODY

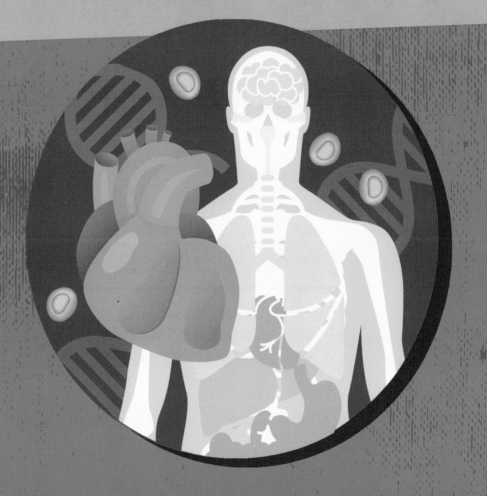

NANCY DICKMANN

PowerKiDS press

Published in 2018 by **The Rosen Publishing Group, Inc.**
29 East 21st Street, New York, NY 10010

Cataloging-in-Publication Data
Names: Dickmann, Nancy.
Title: Q & A about the human body / Nancy Dickmann.
Description: New York : PowerKids Press, 2018. | Series: Curious nature | Includes index.
Identifiers: ISBN 9781499433937 (pbk.) | ISBN 9781499433876 (library bound) | ISBN 9781499433753 (6 pack)
Subjects: LCSH: Human body--Juvenile literature. | Human anatomy--Juvenile literature. | Human biology--
    Juvenile literature.
Classification: LCC QP37.D54 2018 | DDC 612--dc23

For Brown Bear Books Ltd:
Text and Editor: Nancy Dickmann
Editorial Director: Lindsey Lowe
Children's Publisher: Anne O'Daly
Design Manager: Keith Davis
Designer and Illustrator: Supriya Sahai
Picture Manager: Sophie Mortimer
Concept development: Square and Circus/Brown Bear Books Ltd

Picture Credits: All photographs copyright Shutterstock except page 10 Thinkstock, and page 19 NOAA Photo Library.

Brown Bear Books has made every attempt to contact the copyright holder.
If anyone has any information please contact licensing@brownbearbooks.co.uk

Manufactured in the United States of America

CPSIA Compliance Information: Batch BS17PK: For Further Information contact Rosen Publishing, New York, New York at 1-800-237-9932.

CONTENTS

HOW DOES MY BODY WORK?

Your body is amazing. It can walk, run, and dance. Your body can whisper, shout, and sing. It can turn food into energy. It can think and remember. It even knows exactly how to grow and develop.

All of these things are controlled by one incredible organ: your brain! Your brain is like a powerful computer. It takes in messages from body parts, such as your eyes or ears. Then it tells the body what to do.

PARTS OF THE BODY

Your body is made of tiny building blocks called cells. Groups of similar cells join together. They form tissues. Some tissues join together to make organs. Your heart, lungs, and stomach are all organs.

THINK ABOUT IT

Sometimes, you decide what your body does. You decide to use your hand to pick up a book. But you don't have to tell your heart to beat, or your lungs to breathe. Your brain controls these things without you thinking about them. It even works when you are asleep!

WHAT IS A NERVE?

Your brain doesn't do everything by itself. It is connected to the spinal cord. This cord runs down your back. Nerve cells are a special type of cell. Bundles of them come out of the spinal cord. They form a network that goes through your whole body.

The nerves act like wires that carry electricity. They take messages from the brain to the rest of your body. They also take messages from your body back to your brain.

INSTANT MESSAGES
Nerves send messages very quickly. The signals can travel at 240 miles (386 km) per hour. That's faster than a race car!

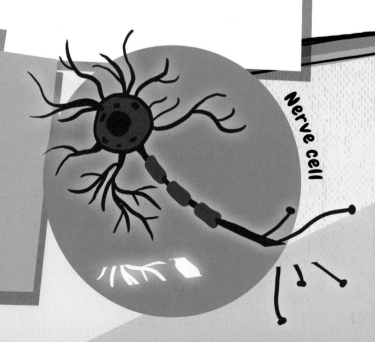

Nerve cell

Nerves in your fingers send messages about things that you touch.

SENDING A MESSAGE

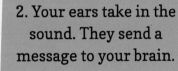

1. Your teacher asks you to stand up. The sound travels across the room.

2. Your ears take in the sound. They send a message to your brain.

3. Your brain receives the message. It decides what to do. Then it sends out a message.

4. Nerves carry the message to your leg muscles. The muscles pull on your bones to make you stand up.

HOW MANY BONES DO I HAVE?

That depends on how old you are! A baby has about 300 bones when it is born. Some of these bones fuse together as the baby grows. An adult has only 206 bones. More than half are in the hands and feet.

Your bones make up your skeleton. The skeleton's job is to hold the body up. Without it, you would be too floppy to stand!

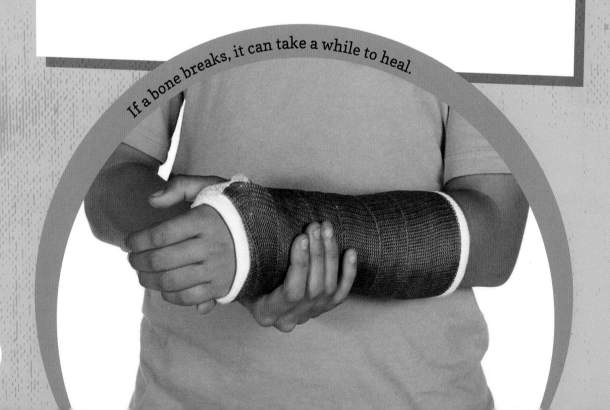

If a bone breaks, it can take a while to heal.

JOINTS

Bones are hard and cannot bend. Your body can only bend at places where bones join together. These places are called joints. Elbows, hips, shoulders, knees, and ankles are joints. Tough, stretchy ligaments hold the bones together.

AMAZING BONES

Your **skull** has 21 bones that are fused together. The jawbone makes 22!

Your body has 12 pairs of **ribs**.

The **femur** is your thighbone. It is the longest bone in the body.

Many muscles attach to your **pelvis.** They let you walk, run, and sit.

Your kneecap is called the **patella**.

Your **ankles** are made of lots of small bones.

HOW DO MUSCLES WORK?

Bones can't move by themselves. Your body needs muscles to move. You have more than 600 muscles. Some are big and others are tiny. Many muscles are attached to bones.

Muscles are made of many thin fibers. They are stretchy, like a rubber band. When a muscle contracts, or gets shorter, it pulls on the bone. This makes the bone move.

A simple smile takes a lot of muscles working together!

SMOOTH MUSCLES

The walls of your stomach are made of smooth muscles. These muscles are not attached to bones. They squeeze to break up food inside the stomach. Other smooth muscles push blood around your body.

HOW MUSCLES MOVE BONES

Muscles can pull, but they can't push. Many muscles work
in pairs. One muscle raises your arm.
Another muscle lowers it.

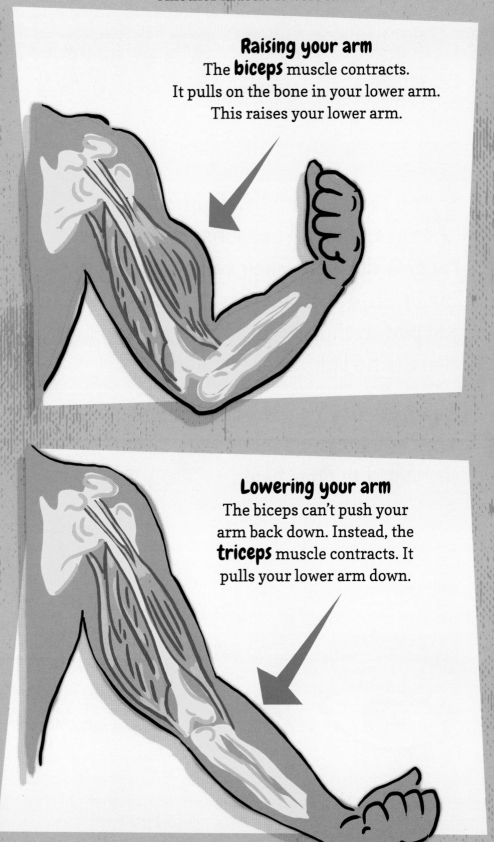

Raising your arm
The **biceps** muscle contracts.
It pulls on the bone in your lower arm.
This raises your lower arm.

Lowering your arm
The biceps can't push your
arm back down. Instead, the
triceps muscle contracts. It
pulls your lower arm down.

11

WHY CAN'T I SEE IN THE DARK?

You see things when light enters your eyes. Special cells inside your eye receive the light. They send a message to the brain. The brain turns these signals into the picture that you see. If it is very dark, there is no light to enter your eyes.

Seeing is one of your five senses. Your senses send messages about the world to your brain.

BROWS AND LASHES

Eyes are delicate, so they must be protected. Eyebrows keep sweat or rain from dripping into your eyes. Eyelashes keep out dust and sand.

THE FIVE SENSES

Your **eyes** take in light. They send a message to your brain.

Your **tongue** gets information about the food you eat. It tells your brain what it tastes like.

Sounds travel through air as invisible waves. Your **ears** pick up these waves. They send them to the brain.

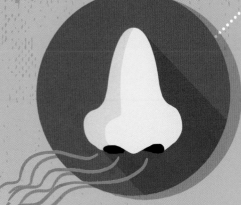

Your **nose** takes in chemicals from the air. It tells your brain about them.

Your **skin** takes in information when you touch something. It tells your brain what it feels like.

Your tongue can tell if food is meaty, sweet, salty, bitter, or sour.

WHY DOES MY STOMACH RUMBLE?

The food you eat goes through the stomach and intestines. These organs are part of your digestive system. Muscles squeeze to keep the food moving. They also help to break it up.

Gases travel through this system, too. When they get squeezed, it makes noise. It sounds like your stomach is growling.

The inside of the small intestine looks like tiny fingers.

BURPING

Gas gets into your digestive system. Some comes in through your mouth. It is also produced when your food is broken down. Your body needs to get rid of the extra gas. Some of it comes out when you burp.

THE DIGESTIVE SYSTEM

You chew food to break it into pieces. Then you swallow it.

The chewed-up food goes down a long tube. It is called the esophagus.

Juices in the stomach help break down the food. The stomach squeezes to mix it all up.

The small intestine separates out the useful parts of the food. They go into your blood.

Anything left over is waste. Your large intestine turns it into poop.

HOW DO I BREATHE?

Humans must breathe to live. Your body needs a gas called oxygen. It is found in the air. Your body uses it to release energy.

You breathe in oxygen through your mouth and nose. It goes down a tube and into your lungs. Your lungs are a bit like balloons. They expand when air goes into them. When the air goes out, they get smaller.

You breathe harder when you are active. This gives your body more oxygen.

HOW BREATHING WORKS

You breathe in air through your **mouth** and **nose**.

The air goes down a **tube**.

You breathe out air and **waste products**.

The tube splits into two parts. One goes into each **lung**.

The tubes split into smaller and smaller **branches**.

There is a **sheet of muscle** below your lungs. It flattens to pull air into your body.

There is a tiny sac at the end of each branch. The sacs are called **alveoli**. They let oxygen from the air move into your blood.

AMAZING ALVEOLI

You have at least 300 million alveoli in your lungs. If they were spread out, they would cover an area as big as a tennis court!

WHAT HAPPENS WHEN MY HEART BEATS?

Put your hand on your chest. Can you feel your heart beating? Its steady rhythm keeps you alive. With each beat, your heart pumps blood around your body. The blood carries oxygen and other things that your cells need.

Blood flows through a network of tubes. They are called blood vessels. Your heart, lungs, and blood vessels work together. They make sure that all your body parts get the supplies they need.

HOW MANY HEARTS?

Most animals have one heart. But a few animals have more. Octopuses and squid have three hearts. Earthworms have five!

INSIDE A HEART

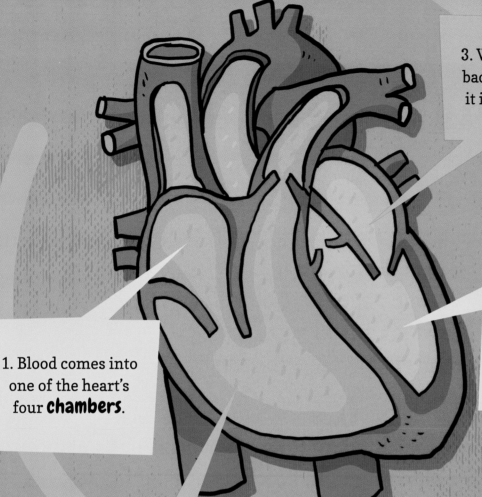

1. Blood comes into one of the heart's four **chambers**.

2. The lower chamber squeezes. It pushes the blood out through a blood vessel. It will travel to the **lungs**.

3. When blood comes back from the lungs, it is rich in **oxygen**.

4. This time the other lower chamber squeezes. Blood pumps out of the heart. It goes to **all parts** of the body.

A blue whale's heart is as big as a car.

WHAT ARE SCABS MADE OF?

Your blood contains tiny cells called platelets. If you cut yourself, you bleed. Platelets help your blood clot. They stick together at the cut to make a plug. A web of thin threads holds them together.

When the clot dries, it forms a scab. The scab protects the cut skin. It keeps germs and dirt out. The skin starts to heal. Eventually the scab falls off and you see the new skin underneath.

A scab forms after you cut your skin.

Platelets are tiny and odd-shaped. They stick together to help blood clot.

20

WHAT BLOOD IS MADE OF

Plasma makes up more than half of your blood. Red blood cells are the other main ingredient. Platelets and white blood cells make up less than 1% of your blood.

Each part of your blood has a job to do.

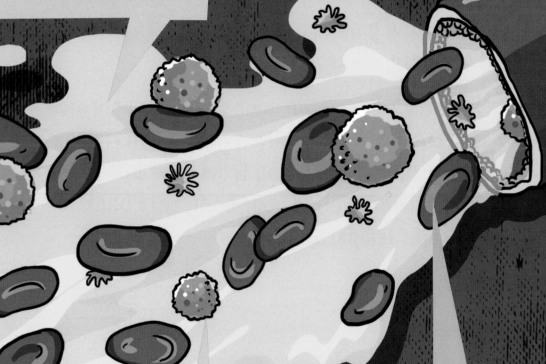

Plasma is the liquid part of blood. It helps blood cells move through your body.

Red blood cells carry oxygen to all parts of the body. They are shaped a bit like doughnuts.

White blood cells keep you from getting sick. They find germs and destroy them.

WHY DO I SWEAT?

You sweat when you are hot. Sweating helps your body cool down. When you sweat, tiny glands in your skin release liquid. It is mostly made of water.

Once the sweat is on your skin, it evaporates. This means it turns into a gas. When it does this, it takes heat away from your body. You stop sweating once your body gets back to the right temperature.

SALTY SWEAT

Sweat also helps your body get rid of waste. Salts and other waste products are in your sweat. They get left behind on your skin when the sweat evaporates. That's why your sweat tastes salty.

Skin sweats to help your body control its **temperature**.

Your skin does a lot of important jobs.

Skin can **feel** heat, cold, pressure, and pain. It can feel if things are rough or smooth. It sends this information to the brain.

Skin is **waterproof**. It keeps our bodies from losing too much water. It keeps water from getting in.

Skin **protects** our bodies. It acts like armor to keep out germs and dirt.

When you have a fever, your body sweats to cool you down.

23

HOW DOES MY BODY FIGHT GERMS?

Germs are tiny living things. Sometimes they get inside your body. Then they make copies of themselves. Germs can make you ill.

Luckily, your body is good at fighting them! White blood cells are one of the main weapons. They are made inside your bones. They attack and kill germs.

When you cough or sneeze, you can pass on germs.

ALLERGIES

Sometimes your body reacts to something harmless. This is called an allergy. Some people are allergic to pollen. When they breathe it in, their body treats it like a germ. It tries to fight it.

A few germs might get past your defenses. If they do, you may get sick.

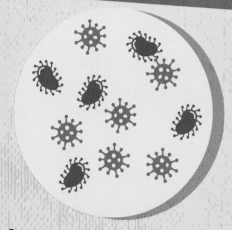

FIGHTING GERMS

Germs can enter through your mouth or nose. They can get in through a cut in your skin.

Small lumps filter out germs. They are called **lymph nodes.**

Sticky **mucus** inside your nose traps some germs.

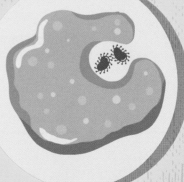

White blood cells attack any germs that get in.

WHAT ARE HORMONES?

Your body doesn't just use nerves to communicate. Chemicals called hormones are another type of message. They keep your body working in the right way.

Hormones tell your heart to beat faster. They tell your bones to grow. They tell your muscles to shiver, to warm you up. Body parts called glands make hormones. Your blood takes hormones where they need to go.

Hormones help a baby grow inside its mother.

DIABETES
The right hormones will keep you healthy. A hormone called insulin controls the sugar in your blood. Too much sugar makes you ill. A person with diabetes doesn't make enough insulin.

26

Each hormone has a job to do.

Two hormones control how much sugar is in your blood.

Some hormones control how fast your cells work.

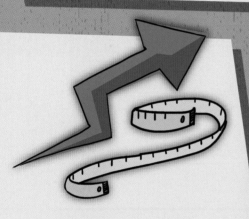

Growth hormones tell your body how and when to grow.

A hormone tells your body when to sleep. It tells it when to wake up.

One hormone helps you react to danger. It makes your heart beat faster. It makes your body produce energy so you can run away.

Grrrrr

27

MAKE A STETHOSCOPE

 Your heart's steady beat keeps you alive. A doctor uses a stethoscope to listen to your heart. It is easy to make your own simple stethoscope. Then try it on your friends!

WHAT YOU NEED

* cardboard tube (from a roll of paper towels)
* funnel
* duct tape
* watch with a second hand or stopwatch

1 Put the funnel into one end of the cardboard tube.

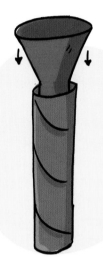

2 Use duct tape to tape them together. Make sure you get a tight seal.

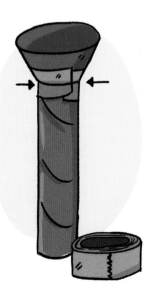

3 Put the funnel end on a friend's chest. Put your ear to the other end. Can you hear the heart beating?

4 Use a watch to time the heartbeat. How many beats can you count in 30 seconds?

5 Ask your friend to do some jumping jacks, or run around for a while.

A doctor listens to your body to find out if anything is wrong.

6 Listen to the heart and time it again. Is it beating faster than before?

TRY IT OUT

Try using your stethoscope on other body parts. Put the funnel on your friend's back. You can listen to their lungs as they breathe. You can also put it on their tummy. You might hear their stomach gurgling and growling.

GLOSSARY

cell tiny unit of life, the building blocks of the human body

contract shrink or get smaller

digestive system group of organs that helps your body break down food and separate out the useful nutrients

energy ability to do work

evaporate turn from a liquid into a gas

expand get bigger or swell up

gland body part that makes liquids, such as hormones, sweat, or tears

intestine long, coiled tube inside your body; food passes through the intestines as it travels through the digestive system

ligament band of tough tissue that connects bones to each other

lung sac-like organ in the chest; lungs absorb oxygen from the air

lymph node small lump of tissue that helps filter out harmful substances; lymph nodes are found in the armpits, neck, and other places

muscle bundle of fibers that can tighten or relax to move bones and other body parts

nerve fiber that carries messages to and from the brain

organ a body part that performs a particular task; the heart, brain, eyes, and lungs are all organs

oxygen gas found in the air that living things need to survive

platelet small particle found in the blood, helps blood clot

sense one of the five ways that the body learns about its surroundings

FURTHER RESOURCES

BOOKS

Amsel, Sheri. *The Everything KIDS' Human Body Book: All You Need to Know about Your Body Systems - From Head to Toe!* Everything Kids. New York: Adams Media, 2012.

Daniels, Patricia, with Christina Wilsdon and Jen Agresta. *Ultimate Bodypedia: An Amazing Inside-Out Tour of the Human Body.* National Geographic Kids. Washington, DC: National Geographic Children's Books, 2014.

Parker, Steve. *A Journey Through the Human Body.* New York: QEB Publishing, 2015.

Walker, Richard. *Human Body.* DK Eyewitness Books. New York: DK Children, 2014.

Wicks, Maris. *Human Body Theater.* New York: First Second, 2015.

WEBSITES

Due to the changing nature of Internet links, PowerKids Press has developed an online list of websites related to the subject of this book. This site is updated regularly.

Please use this link to access the list:
www.powerkidslinks.com/cn/humanbody

INDEX